MW00883986

CON ARTISTRY

CON ARTISTRY

CON ARTISTRY

How to Spot and Deal with a Con Artist to Avoid the Different Types of Scams

Edwin Piers & Instafo

instafo

Copyright © Instafo

All rights reserved.

It is impermissible to reproduce any part of this book without prior consent. All violations will be prosecuted to the fullest extent of the law.

While attempts have been made to verify the information contained within this publication, neither the author nor the publisher assumes any responsibility for errors, omissions, interpretation or usage of the subject matter herein.

This publication contains the opinions and ideas of its author and is intended for informational purpose only. The author and publisher shall in no event be held liable for any loss or other damages incurred from the usage of this publication.

ISBN 978-1-548-00481-1

Printed in the United States of America

First Edition

CONTENTS

CON ARTISTRY

CON ARTISTRY

<u>Chapter 1:</u>

The Art of the Cons

Like a fruit stand overflowing with fruits of every variety, this world is filled with diverse and colorful personalities. So, it stands to reason that there are bound to be some bad apples in the bunch.

It should come as no surprise that there are people who present themselves as trustworthy but have a hidden agenda to deceive you and steal your hard-earned money. Therefore, it is critically important to understand how to identify a "con artist" to avoid becoming a victim.

Con artists get rich by deceiving innocent people. They cheat, lie, and fool people into believing they can provide you with some benefit, when they are the ones who will be making money off of you.

Maybe you just can't imagine falling for one of these schemes. But beware! These guys are professionals at deception.

They have the ability to quickly recognize another's weaknesses, which could be anything from poor health to ignorance or insecurity, and then utilize them as weapons against their victim. These are people who have no conscience or sense of morality and are only out for themselves.

The big question is, how do you recognize a con artist before you fall for one of their tricks?

It is often said that knowledge is power and nowhere is this more true than when protecting yourself against scammers

Gaining knowledge on who con artists are, how they operate, and what common tricks they use will increase your awareness and allow you to better protect yourself.

Once you have the necessary knowledge, you will have a fine-tuned ability to spot a con artist in your midst without giving it much thought.

Disclaimer

Before you proceed any further, it is worthwhile to read through the following warning:

The information and guidance offered here is for informational purposes only and should not be considered legal advice or a substitute for gaining legal advice. The contents herein stated are not intended to be relied upon without legal advice for your personal and particular situation.

Therefore, we recommend that you consult with your lawyer and do not hesitate to contact your local law enforcement if you feel you have been the victim of a crime

<u>Chapter 2</u>:

The Identification of the Cons

The Confidence Artist

Now, who exactly are these con artists anyway? And where are you most likely to encounter them?

Let's take a closer look...

Con artists are individuals who are experts at gaining your trust and confidence; hence, the meaning "confidence artist." They approach you in a variety of ways; through mutual friends, social media, email, phone calls, or simply by ringing your front door or walking up to you on the street.

They come from all family backgrounds; poor to wealthy and broken homes to well-adjusted families. Some are highly-educated while others are not, but they are often very smart. Though they know how to read people and easily associate with others, they lack a social conscience.

When it comes to scams involving megabucks, such as stock trading schemes and fraudulent investment programs, there is no doubt the orchestrators behind them are extremely intelligent. However, some of the best scammers out there are subtle in nature and are not easy to spot.

If you fail to recognize the signs of a con artist at work, you'll be ripped off before you know it!

The Signs of a Con Artist

While it may be difficult to detect a con artist based on their background and by their looks, they often share certain attributes that, if recognized, can bring them under suspicion and put an end to their schemes.

Here are some of the mannerisms and behaviors to be aware of:

.) They are masters of disguise.

Con artists understand that standing out is a great disadvantage to successful scamming. So, they always blend in, by looking and sounding like a normal everyday Joe or Jane.

Also, they usually familiarize themselves with groups (social, political, religious, etc.) and quickly get to know people within the group. By associating this way, they have the avenue to quickly spread the word about their scheme and cash in on unsuspecting members of the group.

ADVICE: When someone seems "too good to be true," or always accepts what you say, do a thorough investigation into the person and their proposals. If you have friends in common, start by asking their opinion.

2.) They have exaggerated credentials.

When evaluating a sales pitch or reviewing a resume, pay close attention to name dropping or detailed credentials which seem too elaborate. Con artists often try to prove themselves by over-inflating their credentials.

ADVICE: Always ask for and check references. Some may even go the extra mile to include false references in their resumes, so ensure you speak to them face-to-face and observe their facial expressions during conversation.

3.) They market unfamiliar products and services.

Many corporate organizations such as banks, brokerage firms, financial houses and planners offer a wide variety of products. This makes it confusing to choose from the right mix for your situation.

To solve this problem, many individuals turn to financial advisers for guidance. Con artists are mindful of this fact and are often eager to look the part and assume full responsibility for your investment choices.

ADVICE: Get all the facts about financial products you are interested in. Stay involved in your finances, and do not entrust all your financial decisions to someone else because of your age or because you feel you are financially inexperienced. If you need one, look for financial advisers, brokers, and financial institutions with a reliable and proven track record.

) They bring out the weakest traits in you.

Professional con artists will always look for a way to bring out the worst traits in you. These negative traits include fear, insecurity, and greed.

How do they do that?

They often try to make you feel incompetent by asking too many confusing questions. That way, you are more inclined to feel you need their services.

Furthermore, con artists will instill fear by warning you about involvement of the police, government, or law enforcement agencies if you don't act right away. Or they may bring up negative outcomes such as destroying a great opportunity, or having your business fail.

ADVICE: If you find yourself in this situation, remember that making business or financial decisions based on fear and emotion is a sure way to become a victim of a scam. Be alert!

.) They are fair weather friends.

Con artists are the quintessential fair weather friend. They will take great interest in you, presenting you with amazing opportunities and promise you the world. They will do everything within their power to make a sale or convince you to make an investment in their business regardless of risk.

But when things start to go south, you will see your "friendship" deteriorate quickly and eventually come to an end.

ADVICE: If you are unable to get your questions answered about a particular product you've bought, this is an indication that you have already been ripped off. Before you make any purchase, make sure you are 100% certain of what you are buying. If you are feeling pressured into making a purchase in any way, walk away. Remember that you can always re-visit making a purchase at a later date.

6.) They look professional and attractive.

Con artists work very hard on their appearance to come off as successful and impressive. They dress professionally, making sure they show off their wealth through impressive-looking offices, luxurious mansions or fancy cars. When contacting you through the mail, their office address will likely bear a powerful and prestigious looking address. They speak with confidence while contacting you by phone.

ADVICE: The best approach is to look beyond the surface and conduct more in-depth analysis either online or by asking close associates. Don't skip this step. Even if you still fall victim to a con, you are more likely to recover your cash if you have done your research beforehand. Don't be dazzled by the effects of smoke and mirrors.

7.) They lavish attention on you.

The politician Edward G. Bulwer-Lytton once said, "A fool flatters himself, a wise man flatters the fool." Con artists know how to use flattery very well. They praise you, lavishing you with admiration, attention, and concern. (Be extra cautious of this if you are a lonely heart looking for love.)

ADVICE: Always confide in a trustworthy friend before making any hasty decisions, or better yet, seek the guidance of a counselor.

.) They exhibit sociopathic tendencies.

One example of sociopathic tendencies is irregular eye contact. Usually, when people engage in conversation, they look each other in the eye and periodically look away in a brief manner. This is not the case with con artists; they maintain an intense gaze without blinking their eyes. This might seem to be a sign of empathy but it is not, it is an effort to intimidate and control you.

ADVICE: If you find yourself in this situation, be bold and look directly into their eyes without blinking. They will look away and hopefully leave you alone.

9.) They will isolate you from friends or family.

Friends and loved ones are great sources of support, but they also can be a voice of reason that can talk you out of making a mistake. Con artists know this, and for this reason, they seek to isolate you in a subtle way from people who may question their dubious plans. They may intercept phone calls or not allow you to contact your family members like a control freak within a relationship.

ADVICE: Never discuss personal information with an unfamiliar person in an isolated place. If necessary, engage a reliable friend. Having another set of eyes and ears will ward off some of their deceptive tendencies; two heads are always better than one.

0.) They will push you to take immediate action.

Anytime someone is forcing you to take immediate action regarding an offer, you can bet you are going to get the short end of the stick. People are more likely to make an unwise decision when under pressure. Con artists take advantage of this by not allowing you the time to think before you act. They push for answers right away without giving you time to consider the offer.

ADVICE: Take your time to think, research, ask questions, and seek advice from reliable third parties.

The One Truth to Know

To save you a lot of headaches, remember this popular adage: "There is no such thing as a free lunch."

In other words, don't go around looking for freebies or else that lunch might come with a big side of scam pie!

When you are told that something is free such as free vacation, free gift, or free meal, be sure to investigate it. Most likely you will end up paying shipping and handling charges or other hidden fees.

Similarly, every investment or business opportunity involve risk. However, if you hear any of the following comments, red flags should go off in your mind:

- "This deal is so real that I invested in it myself."

- "Your return is guaranteed."

- "Everybody who invested in this business did very well."

- "It's 100% free."

- "You have just won a trip, a cruise, a car, etc."

- "This deal is 50% off today only."

- "There is no way you can lose money."

- "I just got a hot tip from an inside source that this offer/stock will not be available for long."

Any person who guarantees a profit and denies the existence of risk is bound to be a scammer and is to be avoided at all costs.

So, take heed!

<u>Chapter 3:</u>

The Lessons of the Cons

Greatest Con Artists of all Time

There have been a few con artists throughout history who became notorious due to the incredible amount of wealth they amassed or how easily they pulled off their impressive cons.

We will now explore some of these infamous con artists and what can be learned from them. Knowing how these masterminds perpetrated their crimes will help ensure you do not become part of another cautionary tale.

The Famous Forger

Frank Abagnale, who started his life as a con at only the age of 16, forged checks and defrauded many financial institutions.

He even pretended to be an airline pilot just to get free airline tickets by taking advantage of airlines that would provide free air transport for pilots who needed to get to another city on short notice. He even pretended to be a doctor and worked as a medical professional for close to a year before being caught. In addition to pulling off these trickeries, he also impersonated a lawyer and a teacher as well.

Abagnale's forgery amounted to over $2.5 million. He was responsible for the infamous scam of printing his own account number on forged bank deposit slips so that all the money being deposited by customers went directly into his account. He garnered up to $40,000 and disappeared before the banks could uncover his ploy.

Eventually, Abagnale was nabbed in France where he spent six months in prison. Then, he was extradited to Sweden where he served another prison sentence for six months. H successfully escaped from the prison in Sweden but was given a twelve years' prison sentence while traveling in the United States. Again, Frank escaped prison by pretending to be an undercover agent of the prison bureau. In New York City, he was nabbed again and returned to jail.

Frank Abagnale was so remarkable, Hollywood even made a movie about him: <u>Catch Me If You Can</u>, starring Leonardo DiCaprio as Abagnale.

<u>LESSON</u>: Frank Abagnale was obviously intelligent and highly skilled in his crafts. Imagine if that intelligence was applied in a positive way! Though he was an imposter and con artist, he eventually used his powers for good with assisting the FBI, and the following lessons should be learned from him:

- Never fear to attempt the unknown.

- Dress and present yourself professionally.

- Always be confident in yourself.

- Be resourceful and make use of your genuine experience.

- Use your natural abilities to compensate your weaknesses.

- Age is just a number; always count on your experience.

The Godfather of Ponzi

Have you ever heard of Ponzi schemes? Charles Ponzi is the originator. He was born in Italy and immigrated to the US where he became one of the most infamous con artists in American history.

Ponzi scheme operations exist today as "make money quick opportunities" that appear to be legitimate businesses but are actually fraudulent.

Charles Ponzi was a university dropout who came to the United States with $2.50 in his pocket. He worked at a restaurant while in the US but was later sacked for swindling customers. He went to Canada where he secured a job at a bank serving mostly Italian immigrants. Coincidentally, the owner of that bank was also a fraudster who was shortchanging customers to cover his own bad debt. When caught, the bank owner fled to Mexico, leaving Ponzi jobless.

After writing fraudulent checks and getting caught up in various criminal activities, Ponzi spent a few years in jail. Upon release, he discovered he could buy foreign postal coupons at a cheap rate in Italy and trade them for US stamps, which could be sold to make a profit.

With a renewed sense of determination, Ponzi collected money from friends and associates and promised them 50% return in 90 days. He then set up a company to raise money from the public to further facilitate this scheme.

The investment scheme became very popular and Ponzi lived lavishly as a result. He was bringing in investors at an astonishing rate. Although the money was flowing, the reality was that he was racking up huge amounts of debt.

Eventually, the public became suspicious and the media started exposing his loopholes. The whole game began to crash as people started demanding their money. Federal agents raided his office, found no stock of stamps, and closed it down. Everyone that had invested money with him lost their investments, and Ponzi himself lost tens of millions of dollars.

After pleading guilty to mail fraud, completing a prison sentence and being deported to his home country, he died a wretched man.

LESSON: Don't allow greed, pride, and egocentric feelings influence the way you run your business. Do what you say you'll do and maintain a high level of integrity. Also, success almost always leads to unwanted attention and pointless legal battles from predatory characters who want a piece of your financial pie; therefore, don't go flaunting your wealth for the entire world to see and ensure you have adequate money to defend and protect yourself.

The Yellow Kid

Known as the "Yellow Kid," Joseph Weil was a well-known con artist of the early 1900's. It is believed that he stole more than $8 million dollars in the course of his business.

While conducting his first job as a debt collector, he found out that his co-workers were collecting their debts but withholding part of the money. Weil saw this as a great opportunity and quickly set up a "protection racket" scheme whereby he would collect a small amount of "hush" money

rom what was owed and would then arrange for the
original debt to be forgiven by threatening violence.

oseph Weil used all sorts of tools to pull off his scams:
gambling on horse races, dishonest oil deals, and real estate
schemes to dupe the innocent and gullible public out of
their life savings. He would change his name frequently just
o keep everyone guessing.

n one particular scheme, he would tell his victim that he
was Dr. Henri Reuel, a foremost geologist who traveled the
lobe as a representative of a big oil company. He would
onvince them to give him their money for investment in
iel.

On another occasion, he would claim to be the director of
he Elysium Development Company, promising his victims
nd and ripping them off in with recording and abstract
es.

Alternatively, he claimed to be a professional chemist who had found a way to copy dollar bills with the promise to increase your wealth. He would take the dollar bills and run away with the stolen money before the cops arrived.

Weil eventually served his time in jail and then lived a normal life in Chicago until he died at 100 years of age.

LESSON: The lesson to learn from this con artist and his tricks is summarized in part of his autobiography. He writes in his own exact words:

> "The desire to get something for nothing has been very costly to many people who have dealt with me and with other con men. But I have found that this is the way it works. The average person, in my estimation, is ninety nine per cent animal and one per cent human. The ninety-nine per cent that is animal causes very little trouble. But the one per cent that is human creates all our woes. When people learn—as I doubt they will—

that they can't get something for nothing, crime will diminish and we shall live in greater harmony."

The Man Who Sold the Eiffel Tower Twice

Any list of the world's greatest con artists would not be complete without mentioning "the man who sold the Eiffel Tower twice."

Victor Lustig is the name. He left his home of Bohemia (present-day Czech Republic) for Paris where he swindled innocent people while traveling from Paris to New York.

Lustig's first con job was selling a printing device that could print $100 bills. He took time and described the device to his gullible victims and told them that the only problem was that it printed only one bill every six hours. Incredibly, some poor soul even paid him over $30,000 for the device in the hopes of making easy money.

His victim soon found out that the device actually contained two hidden $100 bills. Once those two bills "printed," the device would only print blank papers. By the time the blank papers were printing, Lustig was long gone with their money.

How did Lustig sell the Eiffel Tower?

During the post-war recovery era in France, it was extremely costly for the city of Paris to maintain the Eiffel Tower.

On hearing this news, Lustig came up with the brilliant idea to sell it. He forged government documents and invited six private scrap metal companies to a secret meeting to explain that the Parisian government could no longer afford the upkeep of the tower and that it would be broken down and disposed of as scrap.

Furthermore, he emphatically told them to keep the details of the meeting secret to temper public backlash regarding emoval of the tower. He also told the dealers at the meeting that the tower was originally built for a temporary stay and that it was always intended to be removed.

As unbelievable as this may sound, Lustig was a very convincing con artist.

Andre Poisson, one of the scrap dealers, was convinced of the legitimacy of the deal and he paid the money. Upon realizing he had been scammed, Poisson was too ashamed to report the scam to the police and Lustig was able to get away with the money.

After one month, Lustig came back to Paris to attempt the scam again. This time, he was reported but managed to escape before the police arrived to arrest him.

Con artists possess the charisma to convince people to do just about anything they want.

Lustig once convinced Al Capone to make a $50,000 investment with him. He received the money from Capone and stored it in a vault for two months. Then, he returned it giving the excuse that the deal did not go through. Capone was impressed with Lustig's sincerity and gave him $5,000 as compensation for his efforts.

At last, Lustig was arrested and pled guilty to counterfeiting. He spent 20 years behind bars before dying of pneumonia.

Based on his career as a professional con man, Lustig proposed the "Ten Commandments for Con Men" as follows:

- "Be a patient listener."

- "Never look bored."

- "Wait for the other person to reveal any political opinions, then agree with them."

- "Let the other person reveal religious views, then have the same ones."

- "Hint at sex talk, but never follow it up unless the other person shows strong interest."

- "Never discuss illness, unless some special concern is shown."

- "Never pry into a person's personal circumstances (they will tell you all eventually)."

- "Never boast – just let your patience be quietly obvious."

- "Never be untidy."

- "Never get drunk."

<u>LESSON</u>: By paying close attention to this list, you can learn how to better protect yourself from scammers. If somebody is trying to take advantage of you, they will likely be in agreement with anything you say. So, watch out for this as a red flag, and trust your instincts!

Chapter 4:

The Techniques of the Cons

The Trickster's Tactics

Presented below are common techniques that con artists keep up their sleeve to manipulate their unsuspecting victims into falling for their schemes.

Con artists will either offer up an easy way to make a fortune or they will play upon your greatest fears. They may even do both to maximize the manipulation! In order to accomplish their nefarious intentions, they will engage in the following:

- They will play on your intelligence and understanding.

- They will gain your trust and confidence in dealing with them.

- They will require the utmost secrecy in all areas of the deal.

- They will constantly reassure and convince you of their sincerity.

- They will deter you from questioning their scheme too deeply.

Their primary goal is your dependency. They seek to gain your trust and confidence and make you feel that your world is not safe unless they guide you. When you ultimately realize that their promises fall short, the con artist will use your dependency as a threat. They use subtle

ear tactics or even outright threats to ensure your
ooperation.

The Trickster's Method

Iere are the steps they take to perpetrate their evil desires:

STEP 1: The con artist will discern your personality
profile and single out areas of weakness. They will zero
in on your health issues, ego, pride, fears, dreams,
religious faith, or your greed to plot how to best gain
your trust.

STEP 2: They will make themselves appear to be the
only one that can fulfill your heart's desires. They will
engage you in a personal discussion and appear very
relatable, as if you have known them for years. If you
seem skeptical of their charms, they may use
intimidation to gain your cooperation.

<u>STEP 3</u>: Their final move is to "close the deal," and get you to part with something valuable you own (like money). To achieve this, the con artist will use whatever threats necessary to instill fear and put you in an emotionally imbalanced state. Fearing that resisting will make you look dumb or trying to avoid trouble, yo yield to the pressure.

The result? Your fear and insecurity lead you to become th con artist's latest victim. Like Andre Poisson, you may eve be too ashamed to report the incident to the authorities.

The Trickster's Bag of Tricks

Here are some examples of common threats or excuses co artists use to get their victim's cooperation:

- **Religious Threats**: They may use your religious beliefs against you to make you feel that you are going against your faith if you do not handle the situation the way they want you to.

- **Health-related Threats**: They offer false information that goes against a doctor's orders saying that the doctor only wants to get money from you for expensive treatments. With no means of authenticating the information and the fear and desperation that comes along with health issues, you consider giving an "alternative treatment" a shot.

- **Banking Threats**: If the con involves dealing with banks, they might tell you not to speak with the bankers. They will use the excuse that they are offering such a spectacular deal that the bankers will deny it exists simply because they don't want to lose business.

- **"Time is of the essence" Threat**: The con artist requires that you act now, or there will be repercussions. Beware of this powerful phrase: "Last chance, act now!" Con artists frequently use time-pressure techniques to get their way.

- **Labeling/Gossip Threats**: You probably see this on the news where somebody uses negative labels (racist, bigot, sexist, unpatriotic, rude and offensive etc.) against another person in an attempt to win and end all arguments, throwing away logic and facts. Just the mentioning of these labels often makes the accused back off and agree with the accuser. This is a modern equivalent to the old days where anybody who disagreed with the church was accused of "blasphemy" or being a "witch" during the Reformation, just so the public would turn against them. Con artists often threaten to spread false gossip about you unless you give in to what they want. (Fortunately, there are defamation laws against these types of things; unfortunately, you will then need to be wary of falling for a potential lawyer's con.)

Though these are only a few examples, the list of possible threats and excuses is endless, each designed to appeal to our innermost desires and fears. If you fall victim to their harms and threats, you risk giving away your control of our life.

<u>Chapter 5</u>:

The Games of the Cons

Common Modern Day Scams

Con artists are always coming up with new ideas, and changes in laws and new innovations provide them with the environment they need to work around, create, and perpetrate original tricks.

Although it would be impossible to list every scam under the sun, many of them generally fall into broad categories—street scams, money scams, internet scams, relationship/dating scams, etc.—and for the purpose of prevention, it certainly helps to categorize them into groups

Here are some examples along with some common schemes you may encounter.

Street Scams

With cons that take place in public, you will find out that it usually involves a small amount of money and the victim is usually approached by a stranger who convinces them to make a bet. An example of these are:

.) Three-card Monte

This is one of the famous street-con games out there. The con convinces bystanders to wager a bet on a simple card game. The con artist lays three playing cards in the front of the victim, flipping one card over to reveal what it is. Then the con artist quickly rearranges the cards on the table. The victim wins the bet if the correct card is picked.

Sounds like a simple game, right? It's actually not as simple as it seems. The con artist is a master of sleight of hand and distraction and knows how to switch the cards without the victim noticing.

In reality, the con artist is the one who has control calling all the shots. They may allow the victim to win few rounds to pull them in, but will turn the tables and take as much money from the victim as possible. (Talk about *"all in"* for the final poker game.)

2.) Street Hustling

Panhandling is a common problem, especially in metropolitan areas, where an individual solicits money from pedestrians as charity for the less fortunate. While some panhandlers are legitimately down on their luck, others are street hustlers, looking to fool people and steal money from unsuspecting victims.

These con artists will choose different locations that get heavy foot traffic and make up some sob story claiming to be homeless to take advantage of others' good-hearted nature. Or sometimes they are even aggressive, annoying their targeted victims until they get whatever they want (aggressive panhandling is illegal by the way).

Another variation of this scam is when someone creates a fake charity and asks for donations on the street. Some con artists would even go to the extreme of illegitimately posing as a legitimate well-known charity. If so, tell them you will donate as a check to the charity's name (never an individual's name), and gauge how that person responds.

ADVICE: If you ever want to give to the less fortunate, do so through a recognized organization and not through random street hustlers.

Investments Scams

Whether you call it a business scam, stock market con, or marketing schemes, they all fall into the category of "get rich quick" investment cons that also take advantage of the confusing rules of stock trading, business accounting, and the general ignorance of these rules by the general public.

1.) Pump and Dump

Using this scheme, con artists make cold calls to people encouraging them to invest in a certain stock that is bound to appreciate. They will offer up information (possibly false) that backs up their claim that this will be a great investment.

In reality, the con artists themselves are major owners of the stock. As more investors buy the stock, the value appreciates. The con artist will then sell his own shares when the price reaches its highest point and will make off with the profits. The stock value crashes and the investors lose their money.

..) Pyramid Schemes

In a pyramid scheme, the con artist starts a company and recruits investors to give them money to "buy" into the business. Picture the con artist as the top of the pyramid with the first investors below. Those investors then go recruit new investors that "buy" into the business as well. The original investor keeps part of the money and passes some up the pyramid.

And on it goes. People pay money to those above in the pyramid and then wait to receive payments from those who sign up underneath them. Obviously, this model cannot sustain itself as there is no way to pay all the investors. The only people making money are those in the highest levels of the pyramid.

However, you are likely to encounter some gray area here involving "multi-level marketing" (MLM) companies that appear similar to a pyramid scheme.

So then, what is the difference between MLM and pyramid scheme?

They both appear to operate the same, but a pyramid scheme doesn't have an actual product (besides being touted as an investment) while MLM does.

Regardless, it's best to just avoid participating in them all together.

Loans and Mortgage Refinance Scams

Credit refinance, mortgages, and other large debts are a great market for con artists.

Since most mortgage and loan companies offer debt clearance services, con artists will offer to invalidate your mortgage payment or other debts in exchange for a huge amount of money as fees. Invalidating your debt means you no longer have to pay for those debts. However, the ertificate they offer you will be useless because it does not make payment on your behalf to get you out of debt.

These scams have become rampant nowadays. The con artists target people who are already deep in a financial crisis and are having a tough time making their mortgage payments. Such people usually have some home equity, a staggering amount of debts, and very little money.

The con artist, being aware of these facts, will offer a loan to the victim, while they target an easy foreclosure on the victim's home.

Online Marketplace Scams

The internet has allowed people to easily buy and sell products through online marketplaces like eBay. However, this also makes them a popular place for scammers.

One scheme targeting sellers is where a scammer will purchase an item and send a check to the seller for an amount that is much greater than the product's cost, for instance, a $4,500 check for a $50 item, claiming because of some banking or payment system rule of only being able to process large minimum balance check.

The scammer asks the seller to cash the check, keep the amount for the product, and send the remaining part of the money to them.

In many cases, the seller will send the check before they have allowed enough time for the buyer's check to clear. If that is the case, the con artist will get a large amount in return (in this example $4,450) and the original check will then bounce.

By accepting the original check, the seller is responsible for the difference and loses money.

Online Dating Scams

With busy lives, more and more people are turning to online dating sites to meet new people and date in the hopes of finding their special someone. But not all meetings arranged through these sites lead to marital bliss; some may lead to emotional or financial disaster.

Sadly, online dating sites have become prime hunting grounds for con artists; therefore, to protect yourself, here are some ways to spot a con artist and tips on what to do in the event you encounter one.

One of the best ways to detect a con artist is to closely examine the content of their profile.

- For the men looking for women, they often claim to be divorced, have a young child or are taking care of an elderly parent. In reality, they are crafting an image that will elicit a sympathetic response from their intended victim.

- For women who are targeting men, they use provocative pictures to attract attention. They usually claim to have no children but live with an aging parent

Some of their profiles are professionally done while others have broken and poorly-written English.

- One red flag to watch for is a profile stating that they are American citizens. Real American citizens do not usually include that information in their profile. Pay close attention to their profile pictures as many con artists cut and paste pictures from other profiles and use it to build their fake online identity.

Going beyond the details of their profile, once you have begun communication, watch for red flags in their behavior

- Con artists will typically say that they feel an instant attraction and are quick to ask for your personal information—email, phone number, address, etc. See, the entire con job is based on their ability to communicate with you outside the confines of the online dating site to get you to pay for some other third-party service to continue chatting with them or to get your information that can be sold to spammers. So be careful about what information you divulge.

ADVICE: If you meet somebody you suspect might be a con artist on a dating site, take these measures:

- Avoid giving out your email address or any other personal information.

- Block the person from having access to view your profile details.

- Report the person and their profile to the site administrator.

- Cease contact and never look back.

Events Scams

Another popular scam involves live events.

The con artist will stand outside an event venue or tourist attraction selling tickets, or they will post the tickets for sale online sites saying they are unable to use them. This is very popular for tickets to theaters, local landmarks, and sporting events.

In reality, the tickets are fake. You will be denied entrance to the event or attraction and will have lost your money.

The trouble is that it is very hard to spot a counterfeit ticket unless you are an expert in that area. Plenty of people have fallen victim to this con. Which is why it is advisable to buy tickets straight from the source or from ticket authorities like Ticketmaster.

Mystery Evaluator Scams

This sophisticated scam has been so successful that it has spread to virtually every nation around the globe. It involves letters sent to consumers offering them a job opportunity evaluating one or more money wire services.

The letter is sent to consumers along with a cashier's check or a hefty sum of money. The letter instructs the recipient to cash the check at a local bank, keep a percentage of the cash as payment for an evaluation of the wire service, and wire the rest of the money to a designated location.

Of course, the unfortunate situation here is that the cashier's check bounces and the victim is held responsible for the money.

Phishing Scams – Fake Calls and Emails

These are cons in which the con artist tricks you into giving out your personal information such as credit card numbers, bank account numbers, or even passwords.

The con artist contacts you through an email, phone call, text message, or social media message claiming to come from a legitimate business such as the bank. Then they request that you provide or confirm your personal details.

- For instance, the con artist may state that the bank is verifying customer details stored in their system because of a technical error that erased their customer data.

- Or they may ask you to participate in a customer survey where you will be asked to divulge personal information.

Another popular scheme is that the con artist will pretend to be calling you on behalf of your credit card company to warn you about suspicious activity on your account.

- They will tell you that a large purchase has been made using your account and ask whether you authorized it. When you answer, they will then ask you to confirm your bank or credit card details so that this purchase can be investigated.

- In some cases, the con artist may already be in possession of your credit card number and will ask you to verify your identity by giving them the security code on the card.

If you provide your personal details to the con artist, they will use those details to perpetrate credit card fraud.

Operation: Foil and Fold

Can you avoid becoming a victim of all these previously mentioned cons?

Yes, you can!

Arming yourself with the information you now know, you have taken the first crucial steps toward protecting yourself

Other practical steps you can take to foil the plans of a con artist are as follows:

- If anybody contacts you through phone or email and offers you money (or a fabulous trip to Tahiti), end the call immediately. Remember that if it seem too good to be true, IT IS!

- On the other hand, if they request money from you always refer them to your attorney or accountant. I you don't have one, just mention the name of a popular attorney or accountant.

- Never give money to a stranger. If you want to donate to charity, research them through www.charitynavigator.org and always give your donation to them directly. Any person demanding your prepaid card details or any type of untraceable payment method is a scam. Never fall for it.

- Never give any money to a business based solely on the likeability or charisma of the salesperson. After all, professional con artists have mastered the art of persuasion through their countless attempted schemes.

Chapter 6:

The Countermeasure of the Cons

Preventing a Con

Let's take it a step further and look at a few more best practices you can take to ensure you maintain total control of your life.

1.) Never be greedy

Who among us wouldn't like to be wealthy? Con artists love to take advantage of their victim's greed and voracious craving for easy wealth. They know when faced with the possibility of great wealth, emotional desire takes over and often overrides common sense. But nothing, absolutely nothing, is free. Any deal that seems too good to be true is bound to be a scam. Be content with what you have, and focus less on what you don't have.

.) Don't accept solicitations

Anytime somebody comes to your door offering to do maintenance or home repairs, shut the door. Or, if you get a cold call for an investment opportunity you know nothing about, hang up the phone. Sure, there are legitimate businesses that offer door-to-door services or make cold calls to get clients and customers. However, you will be better off conducting your own independent research or by asking for referrals from friends or trusted neighbors.

) Secure your personal data

Personal information should be closely guarded. This includes social security numbers, credit card numbers, and bank account details. Whenever you are asked to provide such details, take extra steps to ensure you are dealing with a reputable company. Find out why the information is necessary and how the information will be used. This is very important because if this information falls into the wrong hands, you could have your identity stolen and your bank account drained.

Determining a Con

What makes a con artist unique is their natural ability to manipulate people around them. Using this ability makes them feel powerful over others. As such, they have no regret or remorse over their actions.

Furthermore, con artists possess the natural ability to entertain a lot of issues at the same time – it is easy for them to use different characters, victims, and scam strategies and keep all the details in tact. They can access ny information very quickly and are blessed with exceptional memory.

Does this make a con artist superhuman? Not exactly. But even Superman himself had to respect his mortal enemy, Lex Luthor, for his evil genius abilities. So must you!

A con artist is only as great as its victim.

So, when a potential con artist is encouraging you to buy into the latest trend or take advantage of a limited-time opportunity, you would be wise to ask the following questions depending on the scenario:

- "May I have your business registration number?"

- "May I call your company about this offer?"

- "What agencies of the government are you registered with?"

- "Can you wait while I contact the account holder to further vet the check?"

- "Do you mind if I get a second opinion about your proposal?"

- "I want to see samples of your work."

- "Please provide some references for me to check."

Con artists hate these types of questions! They will either persist with false information or refuse to answer, giving you lots of excuses. Or perhaps they will act defensive by playing the victim card, accusing you of being rude, offensive, intrusive, or whatever "negative" adjective from the dictionary they can think up.

Don't buy into this trickery! You are simply asking questions that an honest person would have no problem answering.

Be firm and shameless in grilling suspected cons, especially if they initially approached you. You have a right to NOT be conned.

Dealing with a Con

Although con artists are usually quite clever at answering questions, sometimes they may be reluctant or even incapable of providing specific details when pressed. So use this to your advantage!

For example, suppose a slick in a fancy suit is pushing to close a huge business deal. It would be prudent to request details such as these:

- Their connection with the investment being discussed and their affiliates.

- The principals of the business and their track record with investors.

- The background information of the promoters and principals of the investment such as work experienc educational history, etc.

- The personal benefit they will gain from your business (i.e., commission or fee income).

When you start asking a con artist a lot of questions, you will notice they will either try to distract you or push you t make a hasty decision on the spot. They do this by employing the "hard sell technique" saying that you must act now to comply with what they wanted you to do in the first place.

If you request the details of any deal in writing, they may get nervous or better yet, leave you alone.

Remember, contracts are con artists' worst enemies and honest people's best friends.

Now then, how do you use this to your advantage when evaluating a deal with somebody you just met? To safeguard your interest, do the following:

- Ask for a written documentation of any offer that is made.

- Ensure you have their real contact information and address, not postal office box.

- Request a valid identification (driver's license) and write it down.

TIP: Make sure you gather this information from them in a polite manner. If they are the real deal, they should have no problem complying with your request.

Exposing a Con

Finally, what do you do when you realized that you have been conned?

Con artists assume their victims are foolish and will be afraid or ashamed to report them to the authorities. Remember that if you are keeping silent after being conne you are giving the con artist the freedom to continue stealing from other innocent people.

So, this is the time to act! If you have found yourself the victim of a con, follow these steps to blow the whistle:

STEP 1: Write down every detail you can remember a soon as possible while they are still fresh in your memory.

STEP 2: Collect any documented proof such as receip phone records, and contracts.

STEP 3: Contact the right authorities. You may have to talk to a few sources to find the right authority who is willing to help you. Among the agencies to contact are:

- Your local police department may have a special unit to handle fraud cases.

- The Better Business Bureau will have records of deceitful businesses.

- Federal agencies such as the Federal Trade Commission, and the Securities and Exchange Commission can help with securities fraud.

f these options do not work out, you may consider ontacting the media or your local television or radio ations. Most of them have investigative reporters who ack down con artists to demand answers and inform the ublic.

<u>Chapter 7:</u>

The End of the Cons

Throughout history, con artists have wreaked havoc on their unsuspecting victims. And technological advancements have unveiled a new breed of con artists who can inflict constantly innovative damages with just a few clicks or phone calls away.

Given the enormous sums of money that can be made from these schemes, con artists will continue their attack until people learn to stop falling for their tricks.

To win against a con artist, you must learn their game. Whether you are negotiating a deal, investing in a business

pportunity, or buying a new product, understanding how a
on artist works will prepare you to thwart their evil plot.

Iowever, simply knowing this information is not enough.
When faced with a decision, pay close attention, ask
uestions, take the time to consider a new opportunity and,
unsure, walk away before you become a victim.

uthor and businessman Ziad K. Abdelnour once said, "Be
ıreful who you trust; the devil was once an angel."

Tow that you are an educated con artist detector, you will
e well prepared when you encounter a devil disguised as an
ıgel, but most importantly, be able to counter it.

CPSIA information can be obtained
at www.ICGtesting.com
Printed in the USA
BVHW041459290820
587582BV00017B/1715